T0060440

STICKER PUZZLES

FOR CREATIVE KIDS

Adventures in Treasure Land

Meet
Ben and **Emma**

Ben and Emma are explorers. They travel all over the world. This time, they are in **Treasure Land**, where mysterious creatures and precious treasures are hidden. Let's go treasure hunting while completing the sticker activity!

Mission

Complete all the treasure activities! Then put the items on the treasure map.

1 Level

Emma and Ben wake up bright and early.

Before they start their journey, they share a sweet treat—

a **delicious doughnut**—at a restaurant.

With full bellies, these friends are ready to explore!

▶ Puzzle stickers: page 25. When you finish the puzzle, add the item sticker to the treasure map on page 23. The item sticker is on page 45.

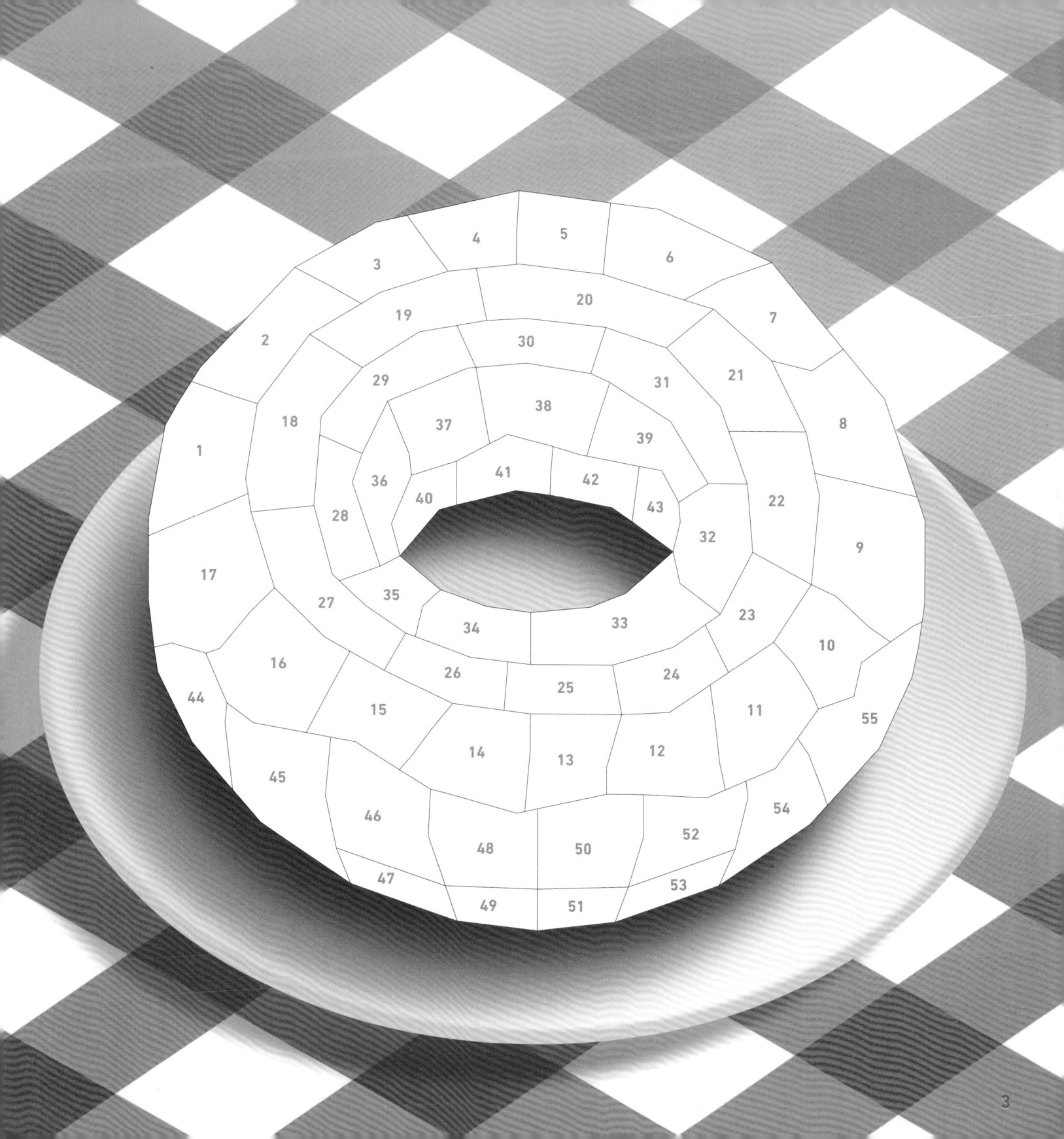
1
2
3
4
5
6
7
8
9
10
11
12
13
14
15
16
17
18
19
20
21
22
23
24
25
26
27
28
29
30
31
32
33
34
35
36
37
38
39
40
41
42
43
44
45
46
47
48
49
50
51
52
53
54
55

2 Level

Up, up, and away!

Emma and Ben fly over Treasure Land

in a big, colorful **hot-air balloon**!

As they float away, they wonder

where they will visit next.

▶ Puzzle stickers: page 27. When you finish the puzzle, add the item sticker to the treasure map on page 23. The item sticker is on page 45.

1
2
3
4
5
6
7
8
9
10
11
12
13
14
15
16
17
18
19
20
21
22
23
24
25
26
27
28
29
30
31
32
33
34
35
36
37
38
39
40
41
42
43
44
45
46
47
48
49
50
51
52
53
54
55
56
57
58
59
60

3 Level

Emma and Ben land in an enchanted garden.

They walk through it and find

a **beautiful flower**. Emma loves the garden,

and even makes a new fairy friend.

▶ Puzzle stickers: page 29. When you finish the puzzle, add the item sticker to the treasure map on page 23. The item sticker is on page 45.

21
22
23
24
9
25
20
8
36
3
37
2
26
10
19
16
7
35
4
18
1
28
27
38
6
5
11
39
56
34
15
29
47
13
12
30
40
17
55
33
14
31
42
41
46
32
54
45
44
43
48
68
53
66
52
51
50
49
57
65
58
67
63
59
64
62
61
60

4 Level

Next stop: the future!

The friends see many modern, high-tech buildings.

Whoosh! A **flying car** whizzes over them.

Ben hopes to take a ride in it, but there is more to explore.

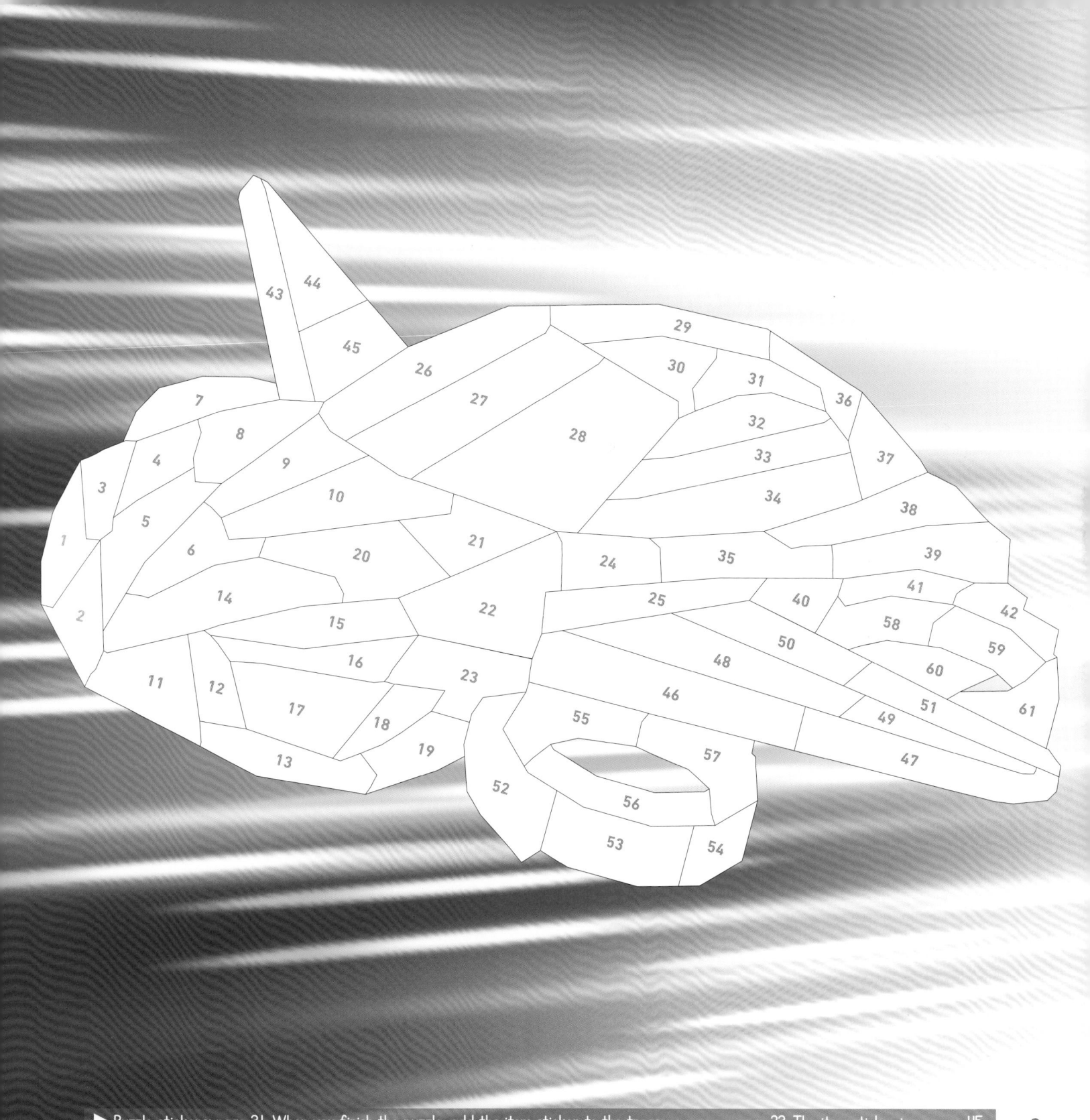

▶ Puzzle stickers: page 31. When you finish the puzzle, add the item sticker to the treasure map on page 23. The item sticker is on page 45.

5 Level

The friends soon find themselves underwater in a big air bubble! They glide through the sea and meet amazing underwater creatures, like this **shiny fish**. They wave before continuing on their journey.

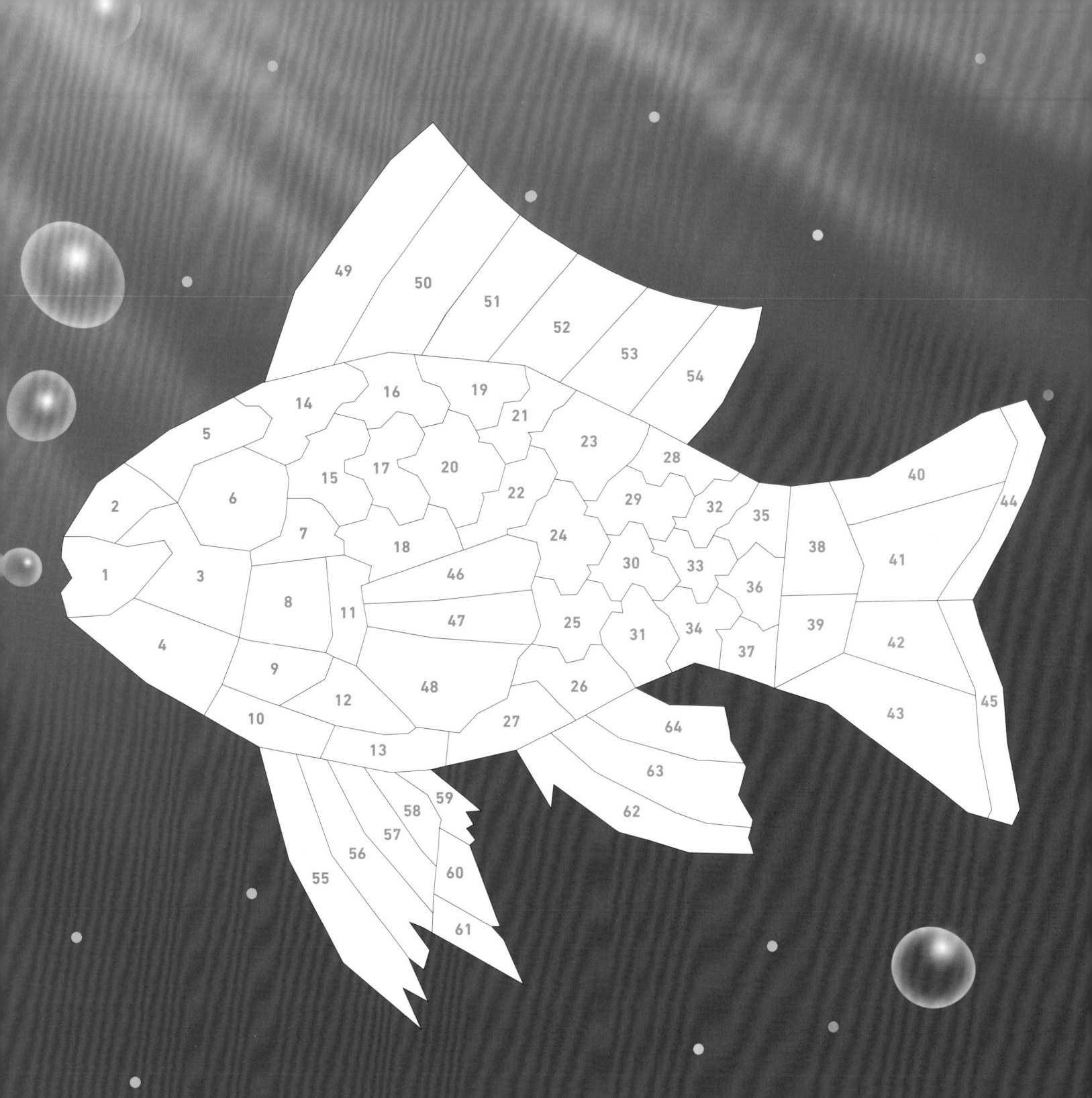

▶ Puzzle stickers: page 33. When you finish the puzzle, add the item sticker to the treasure map on page 23. The item sticker is on page 45.

6 Level

Yum!

Emma and Ben were lost in the woods.

But they followed a candy path to a candy cabin!

The friends gather the candy for a snack

before they continue on their adventure.

▶ Puzzle stickers: page 35. When you finish the puzzle, add the item sticker to the treasure map on page 23. The item sticker is on page 45.

7

Level

While exploring the jungle, Emma and Ben discover a brilliant bird perched on a branch above them. Emma points to the extraordinary eggs nestled in the bird's nest.

▶ Puzzle stickers: page 37. When you finish the puzzle, add the item sticker to the treasure map on page 23. The item sticker is on page 45.

1
2
3
4
5
6
7
8
9
10
11
12
13
14
15
16
17
18
19
20
21
22
23
24
25
26
27
28
29
30
31
32
33
34
35
36
37
38
39
40
41
42
43
44
45
46
47
48
49
50
51
52
53
54
55
56
57
58
59
60
61
62
63
64
65
66
67
68
69
70
71
72
73
74
75
76
77
78
79
80
81
82
83
84
85
86
87

8 Level

Brrr! The friends travel from the hot jungle
to the freezing ice tundra.
They bundle up while exploring this chilly world.
As they put the finishing touches on their snowman,
they wonder who lives in the sparkling **ice castle**.

▶ Puzzle stickers: page 39. When you finish the puzzle, add the item sticker to the treasure map on page 23. The item sticker is on page 45.

1
2
3
4
5
6
7
8
9
10
11
12
13
14
15
16
17
18
19
20
21
22
23
24
25
26
27
28
29
30
31
32
33
34
35
36
37
38
39
40
41
42
43
44
45
46
47
48
49
50
51
52
53
54
55
56
57
58
59
60
61
62
63
64
65
66
67
68
69
70
71
72
73
74
75
76
77
78
79
80
81
82
83
84
85
86
87
88
89
90

9

Level

In the desert,

Emma and Ben find an enchanted lamp. When they rub it,

a glittering **star crown** appears

in the night sky. The friends marvel at it,

and then continue on their way.

▶ Puzzle stickers: page 41. When you finish the puzzle, add the item sticker to the treasure map on page 23. The item sticker is on page 45.

6
13
7
12
5
8
11
9
10
1
2
14
17
3
23
24
25
15
18
30
4
22
26
16
19
29
31
20
21
34
44
45
35
27
28
38
39
40
32
33
43
59
60
46
36
37
50
49
67
51
41
42
58
66
69
68
61
47
48
74
54
55
52
77
78
56
57
80
81
70
83
85
75
79
82
65
71
73
62
84
53
76
86
87
88
72
89
90
91
92
93
94
95
64
63
97
98
99
100
96

10 Level

At the end of their journey,

Emma and Ben encounter a beautiful sight beyond the rainbow.

It's a splendid pegasus

flying over a bright rainbow! They believe

it's the perfect place to end their around-the-world trip.

▶ Puzzle stickers: page 43. When you finish the puzzle, add the item sticker to the treasure map on page 23. The item sticker is on page 45.

1
2
3
4
5
6
7
8
9
10
11
12
13
14
15
16
17
18
19
20
21
22
23
24
25
26
27
28
29
30
31
32
33
34
35
36
37
38
39
40
41
42
43
44
45
46
47
48
49
50
51
52
53
54
55
56
57
58
59
60
61
62
63
64
65
66
67
68
69
70
71
72
73
74
75
76
77
78
79
80
81
82
83
84
85
86
87
88
89
90
91
92
93
94
95
96
97
98
99
100
101
102
103
104
105
106
107
108
109
110
111
112
113
114
115

Treasure Map

Did you enjoy your trip to Treasure Land?

When you finish the puzzles,

put the things you collected along the way

on the treasure map!

You can find the item stickers on page 45.

Stick them wherever you like!

Magical Adventure Memories

These are the things the friends discovered on their adventure.

① Delicious doughnut

② Hot-air balloon

③ Beautiful flower

④ Flying car

⑤ Shiny fish

⑥ Candy cabin

⑦ Brilliant bird

⑧ Ice castle

⑨ Star crown

⑩ Splendid pegasus

From the supervisor

Children love stickers. This is because sticker play is good for their brains! Recognizing and using patterns to create a picture strengthens spatial recognition circuits, such as the parietal lobe. Peeling and placing stickers develops the somatic sensory area. The fun stories nurture a lively imagination. And solving puzzles encourages curiosity. The future is reflected in the sparkling eyes of children who hold this book in their hands for the first time!

Mogi Kenichiro (*Supervisor · neuroscientist*)

Mogi Kenichiro is a neuroscientist from Tokyo, Japan. He is a senior researcher at Sony Computer Science Laboratories, Inc. and lectures at the University of Tokyo and Japan Women's University.

Cover design by Nunotani Chie

Illustrations by NuQ

Supervised by Mogi Kenichiro

For page 3.

54
20
33
48
11
31
49
47
26
39
19
22
44
42
29
32
3
16
35
38
24
18
25
1
14
9
27
36
37
55
46
12
10
30
52
50
45
23
8
40
41
4
15
13
5
34
17
51
2
43
6
53
21
7
28

For page 5.

8
27
49
58
9
26
17
2
24
12
6
16
13
55
31
53
29
18
28
23
19
4
14
47
11
30
35
32
41
38
37
22
44
60
7
25
5
3
1
15
51
21
20
34
10
57
45
48
42
39
33
46
50
59
52
43
36
40
56
54

For page 7.

40
9
50
8
7
61
65
32
28
23
21
24
19
3
2
29
30
13
63
15
34
14
56
57
26
12
68
48
52
43
60
64
51
58
6
25
42
18
17
31
46
10
45
49
36
55
35
33
5
4
66
54
47
11
16
27
53
37
38
20
62
39
41
59
67
1
44
22

For page 9.

7
34
31
40
36
55
41
45
33
32
26
30
25
12
24
8
3
27
22
17
50
44
47
43
61
52
11
49
29
2
46
42
37
53
51
48
60
21
35
38
9
59
58
10
13
4
39
28
14
20
57
1
5
6
54
23
56
16
18
15
19

For page 11.

5
53
2
30
8
17
61
26
49
64
35
40
28
59
20
33
14
47
37
39
9
11
60
32
44
46
18
4
36
1
13
41
12
16
7
22
43
29
21
50
45
42
55
48
10
57
58
62
24
34
63
19
38
15
25
6
3
51
23
52
54
56
27
31

For page 13.

Stick these wherever you'd like!

For page 15.

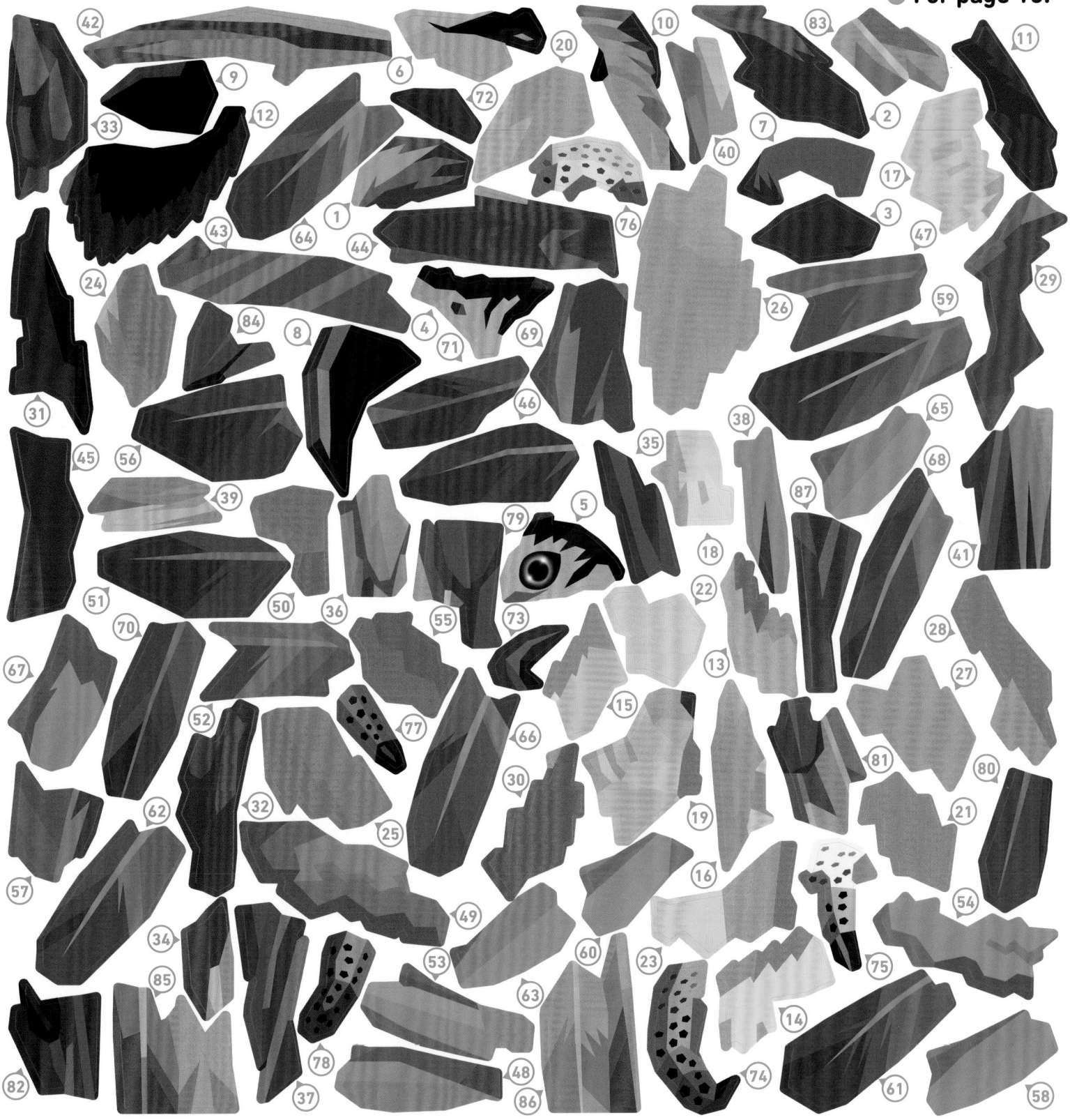
42
9
6
20
10
83
11
33
12
72
2
7
40
17
1
76
3
43
64
44
47
24
84
8
4
71
69
26
59
29
31
46
38
65
45
56
35
68
39
87
5
79
18
41
51
50
36
55
73
22
70
28
67
13
27
52
77
66
15
81
80
62
32
30
19
21
25
57
16
54
49
34
60
23
75
53
85
63
14
78
82
37
48
86
74
61
58

For page 17.

88
19
76
40
3
53
89
15
29
22
64
1
50
27
14
33
26
41
39
17
44
24
48
62
72
56
59
30
16
43
68
55
31
23
71
60
6
9
8
20
52
85
67
25
12
35
38
34
46
74
79
32
58
37
5
63
21
69
82
87
57
10
42
47
7
4
90
86
49
13
11
81
18
51
73
70
45
36
83
78
65
80
84
61
28
77
66
75
54
2

For page 19.

7
65
35
95
1
20
39
29
92
32
6
93
78
18
88
12
41
40
45
67
42
55
100
31
53
80
19
89
33
64
26
4
14
83
69
30
47
57
37
49
75
76
25
48
27
28
54
86
85
22
34
68
23
79
84
87
9
62
15
21
74
8
50
46
90
81
3
59
60
99
38
51
58
73
97
91
44
61
71
16
52
77
82
98
2
43
5
11
13
72
17
63
56
70
10
94
66
96
36
24

For page 21.

21
87
100
3
109
30
113
80
83
110
58
18
56
29
74
28
38
98
86
69
115
4
62
73
41
9
11
16
72
7
78
66
102
17
31
94
52
46
68
96
23
36
15
97
25
22
103
12
90
50
19
84
101
70
79
105
13
35
26
48
5
77
81
6
34
8
76
61
106
95
67
40
85
42
24
57
10
59
104
44
37
71
99
114
93
107
39
49
47
88
32
92
82
91
27
53
33
14
1
64
75
54
2
112
111
20
89
55
65
43
108
45
60
51
63

COLLECTION STICKERS

Place stickers ① to ⑩ on the treasure map.
Put the leftover stickers anywhere you want!